This Christmas Coloring Book
Belongs To:

____

____

Write and Draw to Express Yourself

Date: _____ / ____ / ____

Write and Draw to Express Yourself

Date:

Write and Draw to Express Yourself

Date:

Write and Draw to Express Yourself

Date: _______/_______/_______

Write and Draw to Express Yourself

Date: _____ / ___ / ___

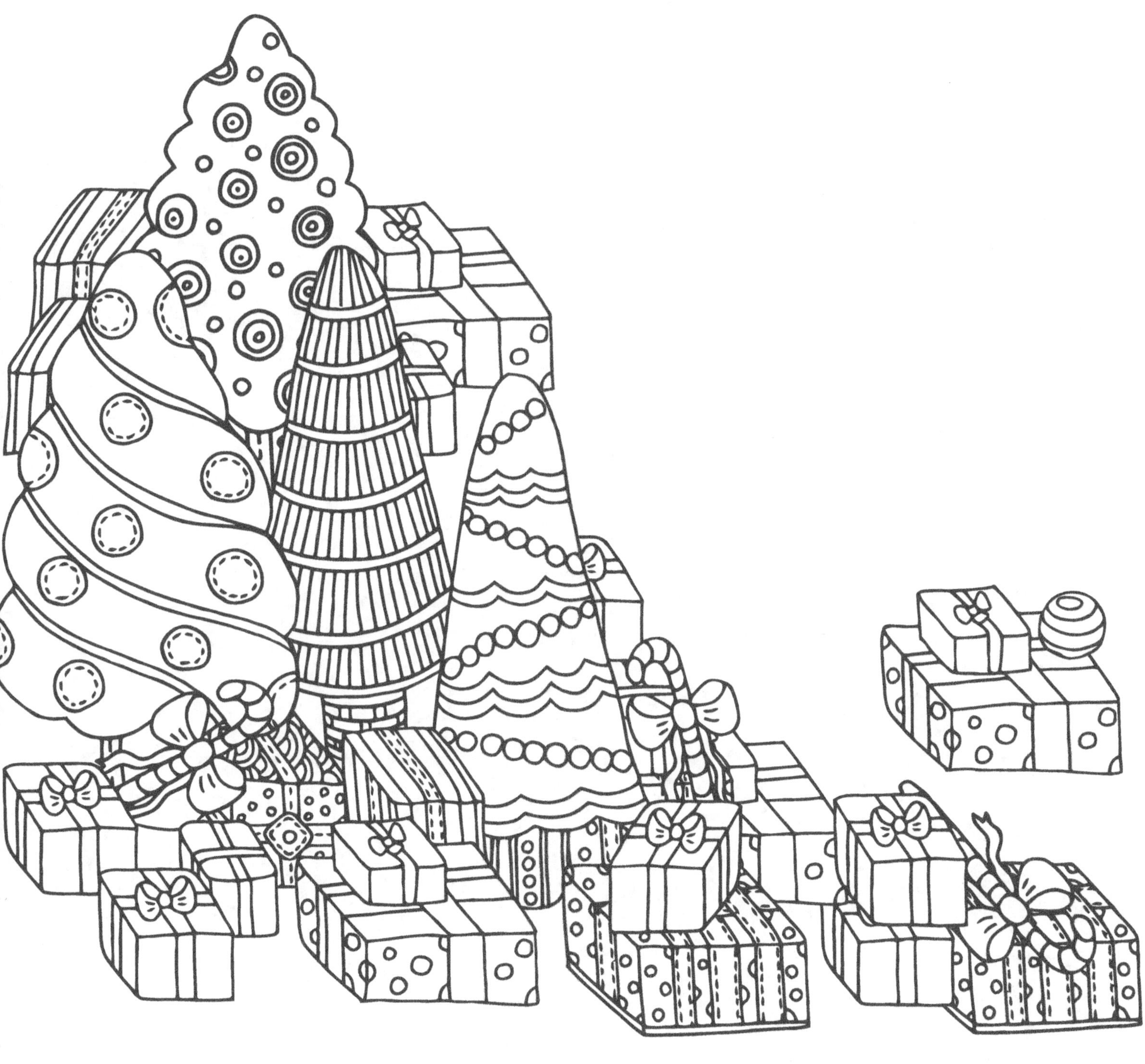

Date: ____/____/____

Write and Draw to Express Yourself

Date: ___ / ___ / ___

Date: _____ / ___ / ___

Write and Draw to Express Yourself

Date:

Date: _____ / _____ /

Write and Draw to Express Yourself

Date:
xmas

Date: _____ / ____ / _______

Date:

Write and Draw to Express Yourself

Date: ___/___/___

Date: _______/____/____

Write and Draw to Express Yourself

Date: ___ / ___ / ___
Christmas
Time

Date: _______ / ____ / ____

Date: _____ / ___ / ___

Write and Draw to Express Yourself

Date: _____ / ____ / ______

Write and Draw to Express Yourself

Date: ___/___/___

Date: ___/___/___

Write and Draw to Express Yourself

Date: ___/___/___

Merry Christmas

Date: _______ / ___ / ______

Write and Draw to Express Yourself

Date: ___/___/___

Write and Draw to Express Yourself

Date: ___/___/___

Date: ___/___/___

Write and Draw to Express Yourself

Date: ___/___/___

Write and Draw to Express Yourself

Date:

Write and Draw to Express Yourself

Date: _____ / ___ / ___

Write and Draw to Express Yourself

Date: ___ / ___ / ___

Date: ____ / ____ / ____

Write and Draw to Express Yourself

Date: /   /

Date: _______ / ___ / ___

Write and Draw to Express Yourself

The
Magic of
Christmas

Write and Draw to Express Yourself

Write and Draw to Express Yourself

Date: ___/___/___

Write and Draw to Express Yourself

Write and Draw to Express Yourself

Date: ___/___/___

Write and Draw to Express Yourself

Date:

Write and Draw to Express Yourself

Date:

Write and Draw to Express Yourself

Date: ___ / ___ / ___

Write and Draw to Express Yourself

Date: _______/____/_______

Write and Draw to Express Yourself

Write and Draw to Express Yourself

peace
&
joy

Date: _______ / _____ / _____

Write and Draw to Express Yourself

Date:

Date: _____ / ___ / ___

Write and Draw to Express Yourself

Date: ___/___/___

Write and Draw to Express Yourself

Date: /   /

Write and Draw to Express Yourself

Date: ____/____/____

Write and Draw to Express Yourself

Date: ___ / ___ / ___

Date: _______ / ____ / ____

Date: ___ / ___ / ___

Date: ___/___/___

Write and Draw to Express Yourself

Date:

Write and Draw to Express Yourself

Date: